Yours

Kakshma Anhad Singh

First Published in May 2021

ISBN: 978-93-5427-732-0

BLUEROSE PUBLISHERS

www.bluerosepublishers.com

info@bluerosepublishers.com

+91 8882 898 898

Cover Design:

Ananya Joshi

Typographic Design:

Ilma Mirza

Distributed by: BlueRose, Amazon, Flipkart

Table of Content

About the poem 'Every Life Has A Story To Tell' 1
EVERY LIFE HAS A STORY TO TELL........................ 3
About the poem 'You'.. 8
YOU – PART I 9
YOU – PART II 12
YOU – PART III.. 14
YOU – PART IV 15
About the poem 'The Sound of Pain' 18
The Sound of Pain 19
About the poem 'Awakening and Invocation'............................ 22
AWAKENING AND INVOCATION............................... 23
About the poem 'Birds of Feather' 28
BIRDS OF FEATHER... 29
About the poem 'I am a Sea and I See'.................................... 32
I AM A SEA AND I SEE 33
About the poem 'Because I Am A Woman' 38
BECAUSE I AM A WOMAN 39
About the poem 'But I Don't Want To Be Strong'................... 44
BUT I DON'T WANT TO BE STRONG........................ 45
About the poem 'All This Will End One Day' 49
ALL THIS WILL END ONE DAY 50
About the poem '*Karma* Never Loses The Address'................. 55
KARMA NEVER LOSES THE ADDRESS 56

About the poem 'Every Life Has A Story To Tell'

Silence is the loudest cry. I wrote this poem just after Sushant Singh Rajput's suicide case, which was followed by media coverage, condolences, hues, and cries. It is always better to light a candle in the dark than to carry out a candle march when the time is gone. Someone who wants to end their precious life would not be conscious enough to contact the suicide prevention helplines. We, as a society are a family to one another. Recognise the warning signs as the suffering person always gives hints. Even if it's not a cry out loud, there is a call for help.

Kindly take them seriously for there is plenty you can do to save a life. WHO gives an estimate of approximately 1 million suicidal deaths in a year excluding the failed attempts, and that is worse. Suicide is a desperate attempt to escape the pain caused by life. Blindfolded by the feelings of loneliness and hopelessness, a person chooses to end it forever. So, let's be that ray of hope to the 'ONE'.

EVERY LIFE HAS A STORY TO TELL

Every life has a different story,
Phases of dark and phases of glory.

Be patient, do listen and do not judge,
Don't use it as a moment to satiate your grudge.

Life has a rainbow of threads that are woven,
What's more important is the road not taken.

Every life has a different description,
Please stay away from assumption and perception.

God gave you ears and not brain to hear,
Let him speak without hesitance or fear.

Don't reach till the end at one sight,
Do not turn a plea to plight.

Every life has a different meaning,
For every finger there's a different ring.

Every house has a sugar box and pepperette,
Human has versatile emotions, he's not a puppet.

To you, it must be just a conversation,
But might save lives if heard with devotion.

Every life has a story to tell,
Just hear, Just hold, Just ring the bell.

While you hear him, pour the care essence,
Make it a pleasure to know and not a condolence.

Life is not bikeable for everyone every day,
Like hair, do live from bald to grey.

One day it might be a three-ring circus,
The other day, it's grave silent but pus.

Every life has a different emotion,
No judgement you make given on a notion.

You listen, you smile and grieve with him,
If not the sun, from dark to dim.

From dim the sun is not so far,
You'll heal a wound and what's left a scar.

Don't be bargainous while buying him time,
It might cost him his whole lifetime.

Sublime it is to be his one,
To hold his hand and show him the sun.

Every life has a different goal,
Don't scowl, don't mend, just play the role.

If you can't change, If you can't edit,
Don't let there be a carbon credit.

If she's a cougar, if he's a devil,
He had his reasons; she lived her evil.

Every life has a different road,
You might be a fellow or not on board.

Every life has a different song,
For him it's perfect, for you may be wrong.

He might be your lover or a hater,
But might have his reasons much greater.

If not emotions, just listen to words,
You might be saving someone's world.

It may end up in a moment or hour,
It may or may not remove the scar.

But you may become his ladder of life,
Cause not the judgement, humanity you capitalize.

Every life has a story to tell,
Please listen to the alive, not the corpse to yell.

About the poem 'You'

This poem written by me portrays some wonderful characteristics of a human being highlighted by my beloved. For I believe, that even if just a human can be a 'GOOD HUMAN', and justify humanity in this era of sin and negativity, called 'the *Kalyuga*'. He can contribute enough towards the whole idea behind the creation of humanity. Principles, faith, belief, and good actions can make it everything pleasant around you and the world a better place to live in.

YOU – PART I

I walk alone towards the end,
The end that has another origin.
And see your eyes see me,
See me with ignited vision.

The hopefulness you hold,
You hold the strength of trust.
Trust in his creation,
Who made it from core to crust.

The faithful trust you have
Has made you this composed.
You know his will is higher,
How high the coin is tossed.

You believe that life is a motion,
Motion that goes on.
The swings are swings by end,
And not a settled stone.

Destruction is for you,
For you the sun is night.
No man do you believe,
Above Almighty's might.

The restlessness of future
Does not unrest your calm.
You know to feel alive,
If not heart then palm.

The clarity of your thoughts,
Clear does your face reveal.
You believe in the beauty of life,
If patiently we peel.

No God opposes God,
It's all our thoughts and omen.
You say he's solely one
For every life, man, and woman.

Your feet shadow your faith
Like polestar at its place.
You live life to the fullest,
Accept its every face.

You know the heights are high,
And depths of oceans deep.
One must travel through,
What's sown is meant to reap.

The human head does ponder,
Ponder over mist.
You say instore is special,
For all in father's fist.
Destruction and creation,

Are what creator holds.
You say it's always present,
When future he unfolds.

When storm at sea is harsh,
Men like you keep rowing.
Cause when going gets tough,
The tough does get going.

Millions of lives have lived,
From millions of years on earth.
Till date man fails to believe,
That death belongs to birth.

YOU – PART II

Away from night, away from days,
You are like sunshine in dusky ways.

Apart from the world, apart from men,
You hail in God's name, Amen.

Above all people, above all souls,
You are the choicest gem the world holds.

Beyond all miracles, beyond all hopes,
You show the mankind discussed by popes,

Deeper than coulee, deeper than crevasse,
Truth in your heart is too deep to embrace.

True to alive, true to grave,
As does the water, so do you behave.

Generations will come, generations went,
Men like you do change the trend.

Be it the base, or be it the range,
Minstrel is you; the chorus won't change.

There lies in a poor, there stands in a rake,
Your heart will judge the flatter and fake.

Not a populist, not a sage,
You're just human in an inhuman age.

Perfect than ideals, generous than thoughts,
Wish you were the world, whether Indian or Scots.

Beautiful than sunrise, beautiful than earth,
Souls like you pay fully for birth.

Above all rhythms, above all stories,
Men like you show lamp to glories.

Fearless to creation, fearless to destruction,
Your deeds and acts are above incarnation.

Clearer to ripples, clearer to trans,
You stand the same, instance or glance.

Brighter than fire, crystalline than reflection,
No one is you post or perception.

Closer to soul, closer to breath,
You live in me, which has no death.

Defy all myth, defy all illusions,
You spread the essence of emotional fusions.

To be you were, to be you are,
Is a thought so far, just so far.

YOU – PART III

My young wish always wanted to know,
What makes the sun and moon to glow?

The sky I saw came down to me,
As if God heard my fantasy.

There was something I asked my mum.
Who made the universe, the moon, and the sun?

She said he stays above the earth,
And he's who plans death and birth.

I asked who'll show me life so glee,
That death I would never want to see.

She said there is someone underneath universe,
Whom when I meet will complete this verse.

Then…

You came to me as heaven's light,
Changed my destiny and its sight,

Enlightened my life like the above sky,
Taught my ecstasy to pacify.

Then I came to know mum's word,
Cause my God created my world…

YOU – PART IV

I thank you for the man you are,
You found me, I could not so far.

I thank you for all the good you do,
You teach me right and to stick to.

I thank you for the lessons you give,
To make me perfect enough to live.

I thank you for the soul in you,
Humanity will learn to be from you.

I thank you for the smile divine,
It cures and strengthens the soul of mine.

I thank you for the love you in store,
That's how I love myself to core.

I thank you for you belong to me,
I owe to God my life with glee.

I thank you for the rules you make,
You give to all with none to take.

I thank you for the flaws you told,
You make me shine like purer gold.

I thank you for the touch of yours,
To me it's love, blessing and cure.

I thank you for the moments we share,
With selfless love and boundless care.]

I thank you for you held my hand,
Come what may, by my side you stand.

I thank you for the faith in your eyes,
That shows me a new sunrise.

I thank you for the power you show,
Empower me to excel to grow.

I thank you for your selfless love, my love,
That's divinity of love and much above.

About the poem 'The Sound of Pain'

This poem describes the 'sound of pain'. The pain caused by feelings, emotions and the trauma caused by loss of love and separation which cannot be described in words. It is the most stabbing pain and yet no matter how hard one cries, the others cannot understand what the aggrieved goes through. So here, I pen down the irony of the most painful loud cry which is heard by none. The battle is all yours.

The Sound of Pain

Mysterious is the sound of pain,
You say you feel you go insane.

No man has gotten those fine good ears,
No live, no dead, no ghost does hear.

The heart, the flesh, the brim if tears,
The pain is breath and breath you bear.

You tell, you shout, you scream aloud;
You split the ground; you groan at cloud.

The sound of pain that lies inside you
Won't bother even one despite cry and hue,

Because it's the sound of wounds that bleed
Inside your heart, your flesh down deep.

The sound is that of a catastrophe,
It's deep, it's sharp, and a sign of

The sign of a shattering universe
The end of your desires and the verse,

The dark pain of emptiness.
The endless doom, the entangled tress,

How hard it is to let go off,
That took me from the sea to trough.

The pain that travels through your nerves,
With no justice to fragile curves.

It slaughters the heart, the mind, the soul,
And leaves you mourning, smashed and sole.

But yes, there's you to cater yourself
In scattered pieces of your murdered self.

A patch of dried blood of you is all
With a cold flesh and an evaporated soul.

You tell, you shout, you scream aloud,
Gather yourself with you covered in shroud.

Because you were you before the end,
The end of love, some vows my friend.

Now the onus is on the eyes,
The tears fall and break the ice.

They hold in them the salt you see,
Because they transform the trough to sea.

About the poem 'Awakening and Invocation'

The year 2019 saw the outbreak of the global pandemic COVID-19. It witnessed fear, panic, collapsing governments, crashing economies and havoc of piling corpses. The door was crashed open with no sign or sound. World at large is still battling with nature's wrath that has caused widespread disaster, and loss of life and property. God has conveyed that we humans are a part of nature and not the masters. Through this rhyme of mine, I plead the Almighty for mercy as we have learnt the lesson taught to us the harder way.

AWAKENING AND INVOCATION

O God, I see you are teaching a lesson,
But pain is deep, Lord diminish, please lessen.

Liberate the mankind of its sins,
They are a part of you in human skin.

Agree I do, to the values depleted,
Agree I do, to mischiefs repeated.

But you created the man and this earth,
To you we own our death and birth.

We bow in front of thee my Lord,
Show some mercy, hold me, O God!

I know you didn't descend me for this,
The deeds we did, you do dismiss.

The earth never belonged to us,
By us it was to be earned thus.

We failed to be the model humans,
You cursed our creation and those omens.

We had no right to destroy what you made,
All the vows of humanity we betrayed.

To climb the ladder of success so high,
We couldn't see at what cost we buy.

We buy the happiness of worldly pleasures,
We buy the luxury and all the leisures.

By fateful ways and means we bought,
And let the mother nature die and rot.

We failed to stand all tests of time,
Blunders are ours and also mine.

But you are the supreme power divine,

Mercy I plead through my rhyme.

Give me another sunrise to rise,

Give me a chance, though you agonise.

Give me your lap to lay again,

Away from dark, away from pain.

Let me breathe again in your air,

Let me learn the means that are fair.

The threads of relationships entangled,

And the humanitarian values are strangled.

Give me a chance to untangle the tangible,

And reach out to rectify the truth, the intangible.

All the abstracts and all the tracks,

Which we kept lay on dusty racks.

We plead for the shower of mercy of thee

To make it a place beautiful to glee.

Give me sometime your hand once more,

I'd live the moments, not count the score.

Send to me your love O Father,

I pledge, all broken pieces I'll gather.

The ladder that brought me to this hell,

Discard, deplete, I tell, I yell.

It dared to vanish the human race,

But we rise and shine with your grace.

Now we wish to grow again,

Inside the womb,

And not the tomb.

About the poem 'Birds of Feather'

I wrote this rhyme some ten years back. In childhood, we had heard that birds of a feather, flock together. Here is my rhyme; it carries dual meaning. I am writing it for someone who is like me, closest to me but far apart for now. Also, on a melancholy evening I saw a pair of birds flying high in the sky and I conveyed to them my message, to be delivered to my beloved.

BIRDS OF FEATHER

Today I saw the birds of feather,
Mum told me they flocked together.

I lifted my lid to see the flight
Was struck by glitter at one sight.

Glitter of heading towards the dear,
Fighting the rain her feathers couldn't bear.

She took me down the memory lane
In the woven thoughts of cheer and pain.

What luck she had I thought at once,
She had no estoppel of substance.

Pleaded her thoughts to bother mine,
As to me she was a soul divine.

Asked her to let you know somewhere,
Love whelming heart lied open and bare.

Love has no language and no script,
Knows no boundaries, no restrict.

To tell you my desire in a way,
No one could tell any night or day.

Risking her life to the deadly rain,
She flew not bothering water nor grain.

Cluster of emotions my heart did bear,
The grey sky held no hope to clear.

Conveying to her that deep emotion
And pious beauty of devotion.

My tears did say what I could not,
Enlightened was I to make her spot.

To her I could convey my thought,
My soul could touch what I could not.

I felt her eyes assured to me,
And offered me a sky of glee.

Just solitude could I embrace,
Turning my heart to fireplace.

Surviving the pain I had borne
Led my bare heart bleed when torn.

Together it's beautiful I realise,
Else is haze, sunset or rise.

About the poem 'I am a Sea and I See'

This is a narration of emotions by the sea as it turns dark. The sea has been personified in this rhyme. The sea being a massive water body witnesses different people, creatures, their acts, and emotions and teaches us to bow low for those who come to us with joy, hope and love.

I AM A SEA AND I SEE

The silent sea at night does say,
O Day! Why don't you longer stay?

The sunlit day shows ecstasy
Of young and old their fantasy.

My blue tide goes to touch new shores,
Fearless boundless vibrant roars.

Millions of feet penetrate my flow.
For them, I bend, I lie so low.

I leave the crystalline sand on thine
To peck them with the memories of mine.

The evocative touch I make,
For lifetime with them they take.

I hold a horde of their emotions,
The silent tears, the twirling motions.

I witness the love and faith of people,
The moments of passion on beaches of beetle.

The trust of child who knows no fear,
The creatures on shore that disappear.

I see the sagas of love in making,
But also, the drownings with hopes breaking.

I hold a plethora of tales in my heart,
With tears and laughter in me I restart.

In my lap the sun sets to rest,
Cause I touch the east, I hold the west.

On my coast in the dark, a bright
Ray you see, is called twilight.

They come to see the spectacular view,
I gleam again in the dark from blue.

My waters gaze the starlit sky
Follow the moonlight till goodbye.

They sing, they croon, they summon you
To calm yourself and listen to.

The voice of void your heart bears,
The paranoid heart, the deadly fears.

They tell you it's the sky not me
That shows me dark to all and thee.

So, bother not the world's perception,
They know not you, it's their reflection.

When I lie low, I am God's creation,
Tsunami in me is the Demon's destruction.

My waters are same, the tide decides,
I swallow the whole nations and prides.

I calm, I bend, I do slow down,
The sun comes out with a hope-lit crown.

I told to thee; I touch the east,
Another day with fun and feast.

The rainbow beams touch my skin,
The striking flora, the golden fin.

This marks the start of day and hope,
When sight is lost, hold the rope.

About the poem 'Because I Am A Woman'

'Women' and 'world' can't exist without one another. Despite this, the world treats women as a tool that can be used as per people's sweet wishes. She is expected to play multifaceted roles that cater to society at all the stages of her life. This verse conveys how she is looked upon as in different situations.

BECAUSE I AM A WOMAN

I am a woman
With delicate threads I am woven,
But that's what the world believes,

I am a body
To please everybody,
But that's what the world believes.

I am a soul
Expected to play manifold role,
But that's what the world describes.

I am so weak
When I hide and weep,
But that's what the world describes.

I am a symbol of love
To keep my family above,
That's what the world wants.

I am too fragile
When my tears are cost for your smile,
But that's what the world wants.

I am so strong
When you want me to fight against wrong,
But that's what the world thinks.

I am a thought
When desired I am bought.
But that' s what the world thinks.

I am water
When my dreams you want to slaughter.
But that's what the world believes.

I am a fire
If I fight for desire,
But that's what the world believes.

I am a skin
To please you and your kin,
But that's what the world aspires.

I am a thing
Enslaved with the ring,
But that's what the world aspires.

I am the place
To confide and embrace.
But that's what the world desires.

I am to serve
With heart, blood, and nerve,
But that's what the world desires.

I am the air
Breathing pure,
Exhaling in despair,
But that's what the world does.

I am the kohl
Rimmed to say that all,
But that's what the world does.

I wear the vermillion
To secure me from million,
But that's what the world teaches.

I am the vag
For demons with bag,
But that's what the world doesn't see.

I am a human
Nectar or venom.

I serve you, what you earn,
But that's what the world doesn't learn.

I am a woman,
I am a life,
I am the reason for the existence of life on earth.

My womb is his chosen abode
Where life forms, I give the birth.

About the poem 'But I Don't Want To Be Strong'

Being strong is a badge that you earn by facing all the hardships and still stand strong. This badge makes you the chosen one to face future troubles and to keep on battling. But yes, you have the right to be weak, you absolutely have the right to not be strong. You can choose to be a normal person and not a symbol of strength. It's okay to be saturated, it's okay to say "I'm done". You are not here to be strong. You are here to live, cherish and even grieve. Please, be 'YOU'.

BUT I DON'T WANT TO BE STRONG

'I don't want to be strong'
Too high is the price to be strong,
Too long is the wait of right or wrong,

Too deep is the pain to be borne,
Too deadly is the wave of storm.

Cataclysmic are the circumstances,
Life is a clutter of instances.

To live, to breathe, to keep going on,
Is now to sew a water torn

Life is a monoprint of tattered dreams,
The cobwebbed skylight blocking beams.

No one to hear, no place to vent,
Given up breathing for the 'Lent'.

Humans are just breathing skins,
There's none to hold pals or kins.

I can't be strong, I can't be tough,
These are black holes not patches rough.

I can't be calm; I can't just be,
The silent pre tsunami sea.

I refute to be strong now and more,
Life is a panoramic whore.

The bag of hope hung on nail fragile,
All that surrounds disguise or wile.

Exorbitant is the price of strength.
I see no soul, no life till length.

I bend, I kneel, I give up to live,
Deny to hope, refuse to believe.

I hate to love my own self,
Fate is a witch and life's a spell.

The spellbound soul, let it free!
From the mould of hatred, lust, and flea.

The fire of desire, desire of peace
Burnt me to ashes, cut me to piece.

The knob in dark I held on to
Was a silver spoon in devil's brew.

I want to be weak; I want to be so loved,
I care for a hand; I die to be hugged.

I don't choose to be a woman strong,
It's harsh, it kills, it's been too long.

No moon in day; no thornless rose,
Untangled is love; entangled are vows.

About the poem 'All This Will End One Day'

This is a rhyme, a truth of life that we all lose track of while being a part of this world and its race. We forget the eternal spectrum. Nothing is going to stay with us when our breaths cease. The sunny side of this rhyme is that even if it's the worst phase, this too shall pass as nothing stays, all this will end one day.

ALL THIS WILL END ONE DAY

The love for things,
The solitaire rings,
The wardrobe palette,
Foods dear to palate.
None will live, none will stay.
All this will end one day.

Those dinners out,
Those dressing doubts,
The love for roads,
The water flowed.
None will remain, none will stay.
All this will end one day.

The coffee mugs,
The Cozy hugs,
The rosy way,
The sunlit day.
None will hold, none will stay.
All this will end one day.

The glossy skin,
Glory and win,
The spring of teen,
Where grass is green.
All will fade, none will stay.
All this will end one day.
The locks of hair,
On the face that's fair,
Expensive fragrances,
All extravagances.
None will stay, none will stay.
All this will end one day.

The future hopes,
The rays and ropes,
The plans concrete,
Backfire and defeat.
Cause none will remain, none will stay.
All this will end one day.

The wheels of gold,
New and old,
The massive doors,
The dollar scores.
None will stick, none will stay.
All this will end one day.

The people related,
The moments elated,
The foes that gave,
The words of rave.
None will live, none will stay.
All this will end one day.

The winters cold,
The summers bold,
The truth of one,
The lie to some.
None will rest, none will stay.
All this will end one day.

The love they show,
The hate they grow,
The social norms,
Devastating storms.
None will hold, none will stay.
All this will end one day.

The holiday bag,
The wealth and rag,
The vanity pouch,
The vows that vouch.
None will stay, none will stay.
All this will end one day.

The healthy you
For life to brew
The blood and bone,
Transitory you own.
None will live, none will stay.
All this will end one day.

Bewitching eyes,
Laughter and cries,
The lips that say,
Unsaid and convey.
None will remain, none will stay.
All this will end one day.

The legendary tales
In breath taking vales,
The peace and war,
The sweet and sour.
None will stay, none will stay.
All this will end one day.

No mine, no yours,
It's all VIBGYOR,
The saga of life
To live to strife.
You incarnate
With deeds and fate.

The universe holds the soul in you,
This universe is none but shell
Where the pearl in you does dwell.

Things and riches when betray, this will stay, this will stay.

About the poem '*Karma* Never Loses The Address'

It's an old saying that '*Karma*' never loses the address like the calf that never loses track of its mother. This is so because it is believed that whatever we come across in this lifetime is an outcome of the deeds of our previous birth, *prarabdha*. It is relevant to mention that an evil thought for someone is also a bad deed. People also walk in for past life regression therapies to unravel the mystery. But the science behind all this remains questionable. As a writer, I believe that the veil of past life '*karmas*' is a mere consolation to satiate your inquisitiveness for pain, sorrow, grief and losses you get in this lifetime. Good deeds do pay good and bad begets worse if we fail to mend the chain. So '*karma*' is what we do. Let's not blame it on fate or past, and act virtuous to earn a brighter today and tomorrow. If '*karma*' remembers the address, let us remember the right track.

KARMA NEVER LOSES THE ADDRESS

Do sins bargain?

Glad had we been if they did.
The souls around want to get rid,

Get rid of the huge burden.
Ponderous we move with them laden,

Laden on us from centuries,
We carry with us no memories.

Every day we count again,
We count again whenever in pain.

Have we shed some of it?
Have we shed bit by bit?

But the harder truth reveals.
We earned some more on shoulders and heels,

Earned them as a part of
Part of the good and bad trade off

Remember the Holy Father's words,
It's one wrong against right hundreds.

Eventually we lose the calculation
That's mounting with the incarnation.

The pious beauty of devotion
Makes it an apt consolation.

To pacify the wandering mind,
To satisfy the nerves that grind.

That all you pay is all you earned,
It knows no origin and no end.

It's your '*karma*', it's your sin,
It's been there since you have been.

To pay for this you've got this skin,
'*Karma*' never loses the address,

How far you run, how hard you press.
It follows you beyond the doom,

It leaves no unopened room.
The room is the judgement space

To show your podium prior to the race.
Remember??

That all you pay is all you earned,
But all you earn is an effect of good you burned.

The good that comes from righteous deeds,
Lay like those unwatered seeds.

For you to come wake up again,
Gather the mud, call the rain.

No fate will read the end of pain.
Destiny does let you attain

The trees to bear the fruits you wish
With acts of virtue in your niche.

If your address has been chosen,
Keep the 'good' safe and frozen.

The calculation now comes around,
The right you do makes it bound.

That good you did, good you earn,
Good you pay for life to turn...

So dear *karma*, until I am found,
I'll turn the things other way round!

Cause what goes around comes around.

A tick of clock turns today to yesterday,
A flip of date turns this year to yesteryear.

A thing and everything are prone to change
Except our love that knows no range.

A stop of breath turns live to dead,
Human you loved starts to dread.

People say you are far away,
I can't meet you, no night no day.

But love I have for you is immense,
To meet you and feel you, I have defence.

Even now you live in me each day,
You are there in a different way.

I need you till my ultimate breath,
You gave me life; you'll be till death.

Mom, I am an indispensable part
Of a lovely person that's you, sweetheart.

I miss you and love you every moment,
And receive all love that you sent

In the form of people and incidences
That touches my heart and my senses.

I know you will always be there with me
Until there is God, sky, land, and me.

www.ingramcontent.com/pod-product-compliance
Ingram Content Group UK Ltd.
Pitfield, Milton Keynes, MK11 3LW, UK
UKHW042000190726
13854UKWH00005B/2086

9 789354 277320